08/07/44

P9-CSU-297

0 1021 0227209 7

ON LINE

You Are Here

Jennifer B. Gillis

Rourke
Publishing LLC
Vero Beach, Florida 32964

www.rourkepublishing.com

PHOTO CREDITS: © Webking: cover; © Jami Garrison: page 4; © Aliza Snow: page 5; © Cindy England: page 6; © Peter Gustafson: page 7; © Carolina K Smith: page 8; © CKenneth C. Kirkel: page 19; © Sergey Korotkih: page 20

Editor: Robert Stengard-Olliges

Cover design by Nicola Stratford

Library of Congress Cataloging-in-Publication Data

Gillis, Jennifer Blizin, 1950-
  You are here / Jennifer B. Gillis.
     p. cm. -- (My neighborhood)
  ISBN 1-60044-205-6 (hardcover)
  ISBN 1-59515-554-6 (softcover)
  1. Map reading--Juvenile literature. 2. Maps--Juvenile literature. I. Title.
  GA130.G55 2007
  912.01'4--dc22
                                 2006022170

Printed in the USA

CG/CG

Rourke Publishing

www.rourkepublishing.com – sales@rourkepublishing.com
Post Office Box 3328, Vero Beach, FL 32964

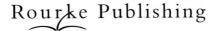

Table of Contents

What Are Maps?

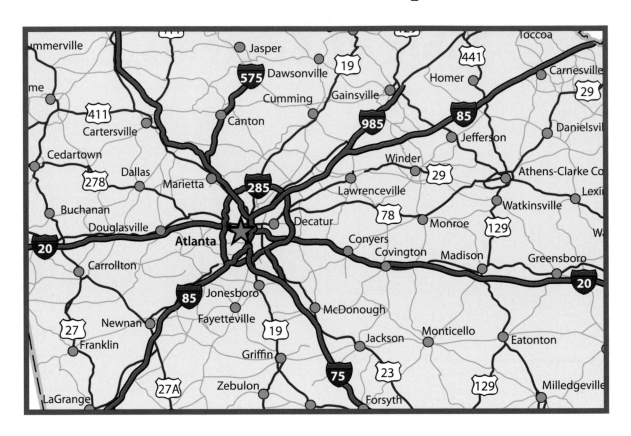

Maps are drawings that show where things are.

Maps can show how to get places. Maps can show how land looks.

Views

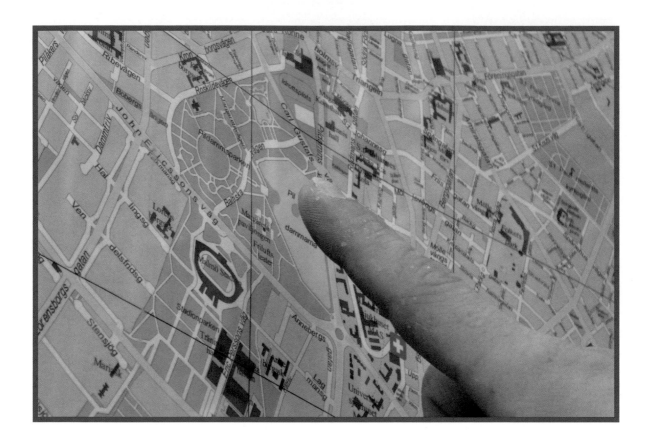

Maps show large **areas**. So, the drawings are small.

This is called a **bird's-eye view**. It is like looking down on the area from above.

Road Maps

Road maps show how to get places. Tiny lines show streets and highways.

Some road maps show just the roads in one area. Others show all the roads in a whole state.

Plans

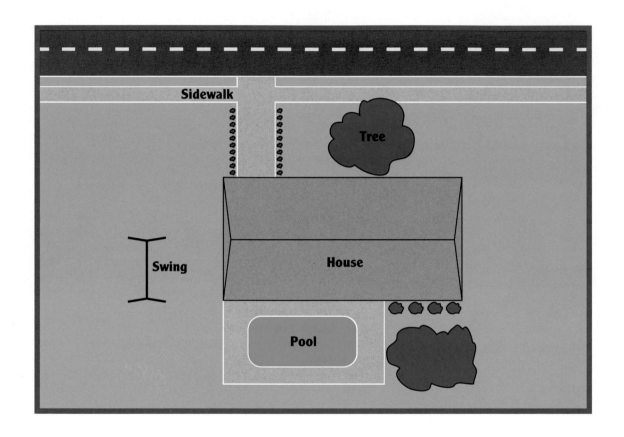

Plans are maps that show where things are.

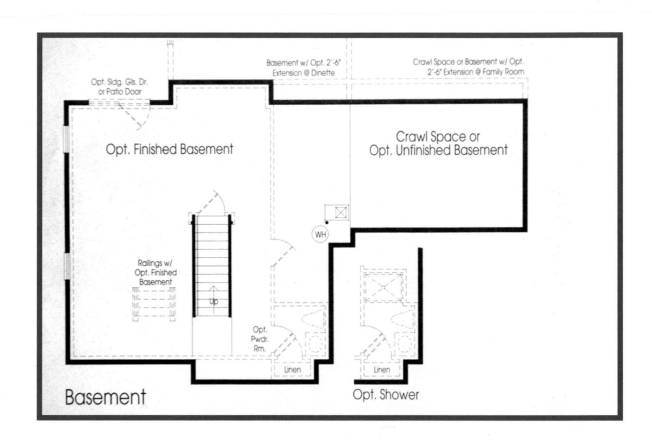

Basement

A **floor plan** shows the rooms in a house. Lines show where each room is.

Left and Right

You need to know directions to use a map. Left and right are two directions.

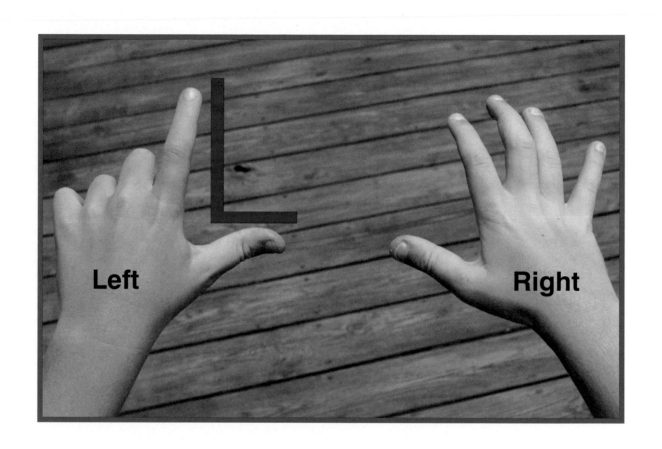

Left

Right

Your left hand makes a letter L. Right is your other hand.

The Compass

A **compass** shows four directions. They are north, south, east, and west.

Maps often have a drawing of a compass. This tells you how to hold the map.

East or West?

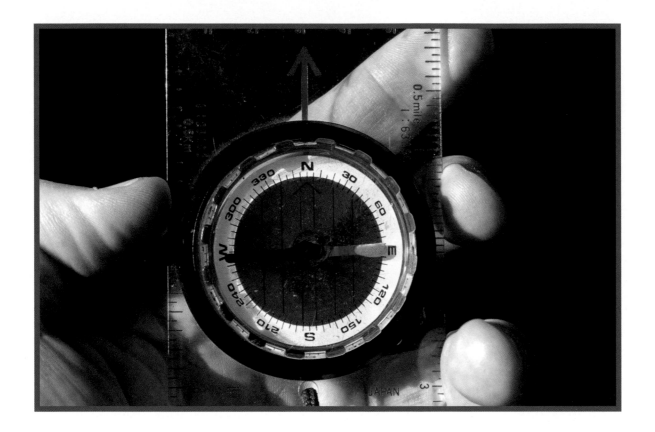

The sun comes up in the east. East is in the direction of the rising sun.

The sun goes down in the west. West is in the direction of the setting sun.

North or South?

North is to the right of the setting sun. North is at the top of a map. South is to the left of the setting sun. South is at the bottom of a map.

Symbols

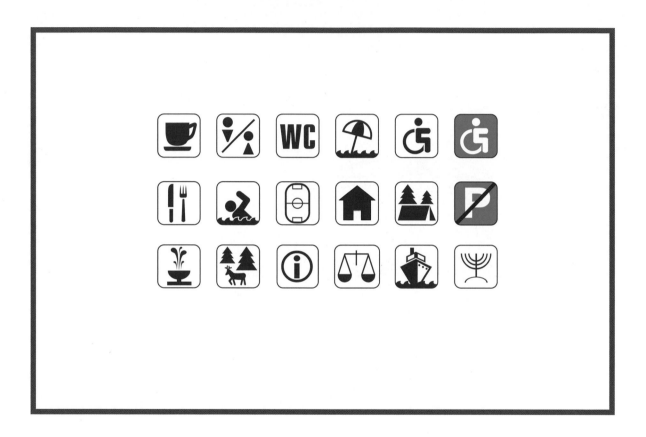

There is often too much to show in a map. So, **mapmakers** use **symbols** for things.

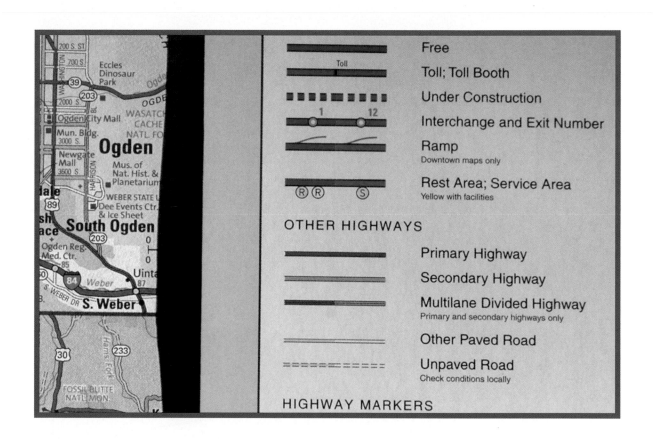

A symbol is a picture that stands for something. A **key** shows what the symbols mean.

Mapping Your Room

You can make a map of your room. What things will your map show? Pretend your paper is your room. Draw each thing that you see.

Glossary

area (AIR ee uh) — land and water in a certain space

bird's-eye view (BURDZ EYE VYOO) — to see all of something as if you were seeing it from high above, as a bird looks down on land

compass (HUHM puhss) — device with a special needle that always points toward the North Pole

floor plan (FLOR PLAN) — drawing that shows all of the rooms in a building

key (KEE) — part of a map that explains what symbols mean

mapmaker (MAP MAKE ur) — person whose job is to make maps

plan (PLAN) — kind of map that shows where a building is or where things are inside a building

road map (ROHD MAP) — type of map that uses colored lines to show streets and highways in a certain place

symbol (SIM buhl) — small picture on a map that stands for such things as cities, towns, mountains, rivers, roads, and so on

Index

FURTHER READING

Coupe, Robert. *Maps and Our World*. Mason Crest, 2005.
Dispezio, Michael. *Map Mania*. Sterling Publishing, 2002.
Wade, Mary. *Types of Maps*. Children's Press, 2003.

WEBSITES TO VISIT

www.earth.google.com
www.greenmap.com
www.nationalgeograhic.com/geospy

ABOUT THE AUTHOR

Jennifer B. Gillis is an author and editor of nonfiction books and poetry for children. A graduate of Gilford College in North Carolina, she has taught foreign language and social studies in North Carolina, Virginia, and Illinois.